Embrace The Ethics

Moral stories of life formation

INTRODUCTION

There are 50 moral stories in this book, by reading which you can gain a lot of knowledge about your life. Everyone is welcome to read the stories, no matter what age. Each story has an instructive title as well as an admonition and motto at the end of the story. If one applies these moral words in his real life, he will surely benefit. It is especially important to tell these stories to young children, so that they get a positive outlook on life. Greetings to all from the bottom of my heart.

Chapter 1

DO YOUR OWN THING, NOT DEPEND ON OTHERS

There was once a king who ordered some of his workers to dig a pond. Once the pond was dug, the king told his people that one person from each household should bring a glass of milk during the night and pour it into the pond. Consequently, when the milk starts flowing, ponds will be full by morning. Everyone went home after receiving the order.

In the middle of the night, one man prepared to drink the milk. Since everyone is bringing milk, he thought he could simply hide a glass of water and pour it into the pond. Due to the darkness, no one will notice. Therefore, he quickly poured the water into the pond and returned. The king visited the pond in the morning and was surprised to see that it was only filled with water. It seems as if everyone thought like the other man, "I don't have to put the milk, someone else will do it."

"You cannot expect others to care for it for you. In contrast, if you don't give it a try, no one else will."

Chapter 2

TAKE CARE OF THE WORLD, DON'T CHANGE IT

As once upon a time, a king ruled an extraordinarily prosperous country. On one occasion, he traveled to some distant regions of his country. After he returned to his palace, he complained that his feet were very painful, since it was the first time he had gone on such a long journey, and the road was very rough and stony. Then he ordered his men to cover all the roads with leather. Definitely, this would need thousands of cows' skin, and would cost a huge amount of money.

The king's wise servant then dared to ask, "Why are you spending that huge amount of money?" "What do you think about cutting a small piece of leather to cover your feet?''

Though surprised, the king eventually agreed to make a shoe for himself.

"This story teaches a valuable lesson: to make this world a happier place to live, you must change yourself - your heart; and not the world."

Chapter 3

ALL OF GOD'S CREATIONS HAVE A GOOD PURPOSE

There were two men walking along on a summer day. As soon as it became too hot to go further, they rested in the shade of an enormous plane tree nearby.

One man, gazing up at the branches, said to the other: "What a useless tree it is.". The tree does not have any fruit or nuts we can eat and its wood is useless for anything."

A tree responded with a rustling sound: "Don't be so ungrateful.". I am shielding you from the sun at this very moment, which is extremely useful. What a bad, worthless person you are!

"It is God's intention for all His creations to be useful. It is forbidden to belittle almighty's blessings in our religions."

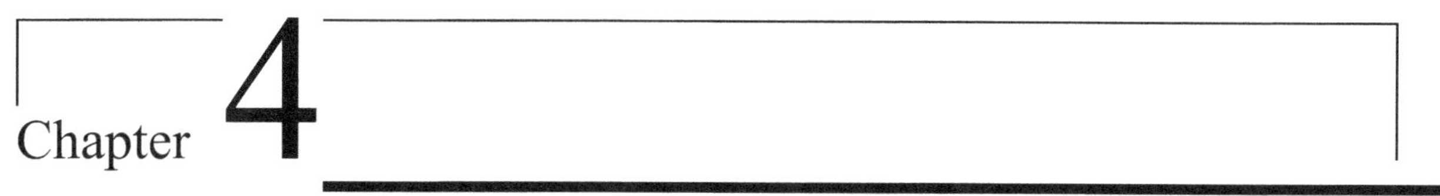

LESSONS FROM MISTAKES

Thomas Edison experimented with two thousand different materials to find a filament for his light bulb. Whenever none of them worked satisfactorily, his assistant complained, "We have wasted our time.". It seems we have learned nothing.

In response, Edison expressed his confidence, "Oh, we have come so far and we have learned so much.". "We now know that there are at least two thousand elements that we cannot use in making a good bulb."

"We learned from this story that we should not be depressed if any mistakes happen, we should learn from this mistake."

Chapter 5

THE CRUEL CONSEQUENCES OF LYING

Once upon a time, there was a shepherd boy who was in charge of a flock of sheep. One day, he felt bored and decided to fool the villagers. So he yelled out, "Help! Wolf! Wolf!

Upon hearing his cries, the villagers rushed out of the village to help the shepherd boy. When they came to him, they asked, "Where is the wolf?"

The shepherd boy laughed loudly and loudly, "Ha, Ha, Ha!" I fooled you all. It was just a trick."

Several days later, the shepherd boy repeated the trick. He once again called out, "Help!" I need help! Wolf! Wolf!"

As the villagers raced up the hill to help him, they found once again that the boy had tricked them. Everyone was furious at his naughty behavior.

Soon after, a wolf took off into the field. The wolf began attacking a sheep, followed by another and another. The shepherd boy ran towards the village screaming, "Help!" Please help! Wolf! Help! Please, somebody!

Upon hearing his cries, the villagers laughed, believing it to be another trick. He called out to his villager, "There is a wolf attacking the sheep." Last time I lied, but this time I am telling the truth!

"Eventually, the villagers went to look. Sure enough, it was true. As they watched the wolf run away, they saw many dead sheep lying on the grass.

"Often-lie-tellers may not be believers, even when they tell the truth."

Chapter 6

THE BAD COMPANY BRINGS HARM

Farmers found that cranes had destroyed their newly sown corn, so one evening they put a net over their field to catch these birds. A stork and a number of cranes were found in the net the next morning when he examined it.

"Please release me," cried the stork, "for I have not eaten your corn, nor have I done you any harm. As you can see, I am a poor innocent stork - a bird that honors his parents. I..

"The farmer, however, cut him short. All this may be true, but I have caught you with those who are destroying my crops, and you must endure the company in which you are found.

"It is said that people are judged by the company they keep."

Chapter 7

SLOW AND STEADILY WINS THE RACE

Once was a tortoise who was made fun of by a hare. “Your pace is so slow that you'll never get far.

Astonished by the hare's behavior, the tortoise said, "Let's race to find out who's the best.”

"The hare laughed and said, "You're kidding!". All right, let's see who reaches the other side of the hill first." Off he ran, leaving the tortoise far behind.

When the tortoise took its time coming long, the hare stopped. It waited and waited until it felt sleepy. He thought, "I'll take a nap." "I can win the race even if she catches up with me," he thought to himself as he lay down under a shady tree.

Passing the hare slowly but steadily, the tortoise continued to walk. When the hare awoke, the tortoise was near the finish line. Even though he ran as fast as he could, he couldn't catch up with the tortoise.

“Racing slowly and steadily can lead to victory.”

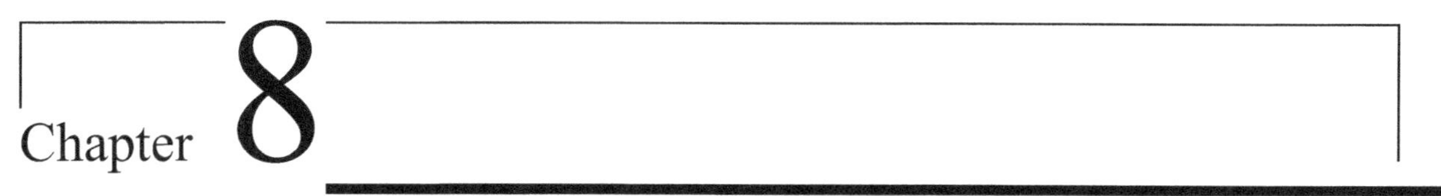

Chapter 8

A GOOD DEEDS DESERVES ANOTHER

An ant found some water one hot day. As she walked around a little, she came to a spring.

She had to climb a blade of grass to reach the spring. When she attempted to climb, she slipped and fell in.

If a dove up a nearby tree had not seen her, she could have drowned. When the dove realized that the ant was in trouble, he plucked off a leaf and dropped it into the water near the struggling ant. As the ant moved towards the leaf, he climbed up it. Immediately after, it carried her into the dry ground.

Meanwhile, nearby, a hunter was throwing out a net towards the dove in order to capture it.

In anticipation of what he was about to do, the ant bit him on the heel. In pain, the hunter dropped the net. The dove flew away to safety.

"Every good action deserves another."

Chapter 9

LIARS AND BOASTERS MAY END UP IN TROUBLE

A long time ago, some sailors set sail on their sailing ship. During their journey, one sailor brought along his pet monkey.

While they were far out at sea, a terrible storm turned their ship upside down. The monkey was sure he would drown when everyone fell into the sea. At that moment, a dolphin appeared and picked him up.

The monkey came down from the dolphin's back once they reached the island. After a puzzled look, the dolphin asked, "Do you know this place?"

The monkey answered, "Yes, I do." Indeed, the king of the island is my friend. I'm a prince!

"Knowing that no one lived on the island, the dolphin said, "Well, well, I guess you're a prince! So, you can be a king now!

"How can I be a king?" the monkey asked."

In response, the dolphin started swimming away, saying, "It's easy.". Being the only creature on this island, you would naturally be king!"

"Those who lie and boast may find themselves in trouble."

Chapter 10

TIT FOR TAT

There was a time when a selfish fox invited a stork to dinner in his hollowed tree. At dusk, the stork went to the fox's house and knocked with its long beak on the door. As the fox opened the door, he called out, "Come in and share my food."

The stork sat down at the table. The food smelled delicious and she was very hungry. As the fox served his soup in shallow bowls, he licked up all the soup quickly. However, the stork was unable to consume any of the food as the bowl was too shallow for her long beak. Stork smiled politely and remained hungry.

In a selfish tone, the fox asked the stork, "Stork, why haven't you eaten your soup?" Is it not to your liking?"

As the stork replied, "Thanks for inviting me for dinner. I appreciate it.". Please join me at my home tomorrow evening for dinner."

The following night, when the fox arrived at the stork's house, he discovered that it was also soup for dinner. The soup was served in tall jugs this time. The stork drank the soup easily, but the fox could not reach into the tall jug. Now it was the fox's turn to go hungry.

"An act of selfishness can backfire on you."

Chapter 11

WISDOM IS GREATER THAN STRENGTH

There was a lamb, one day, grazing with a flock of sheep. After a short while, she discovered some sweet grass at the edge of the field. She kept going farther and farther away from the others.

She was having so much fun that she did not notice a wolf approaching her. When it pounced on her, she was quick to plead, "Please, please don't eat me yet." "My stomach is full of grass." She pleaded, "I will taste much better after a while."

As a result, the wolf sat down and waited. The lamb said, "If you let me dance, then I will digest the grass in my stomach faster." The wolf agreed.

However, the lamb had a new idea while dancing. "Please take the bell off my neck," she said. "If you ring it louder, I can dance even faster."

The wolf took the bell and rang it as loud as he could. When the shepherd heard the bell ringing, he immediately sent his dogs to look for the missing lamb. Barking dogs scared away the wolf and saved the lamb's life.

"Sometimes, the gentle and weak are cleverer than the fierce and strong."

Chapter 12

GRAPES ARE SOUR

During a sunny day, a fox walked through the fields. He soon came to a vineyard. When he got closer, he could see some bunches of juicy grapes.

The fox examined the area carefully. He wanted to make sure he was safe from the hunters. So he went to steal some before anyone discovered him. He jumped upwards, but he was unable to reach the grapes.

He jumped again as far as he could. Unfortunately, he wasn't able to reach them. The grapes were too high!

But he didn't give up. In an effort to reach the grapes, he turned back, ran some steps, and leapt into the air. Still, he was unable to reach them.

He was getting angry as it got darker. Having run and jumped so much, his legs were hurting. He eventually stopped trying.

While walking away, he said to himself, "Those grapes don't really interest me." It must be too sour for me to eat them."

“We may pretend that things are not worth having when we cannot get what we want.”

HARD WORKERS DON'T FAIL

A thirsty crow flew across the fields looking for water on a hot day. She did not find any water. Feeling weak, she almost gave up hope.

Suddenly, a water jug appeared below her. She plunged straight down to see if it contained any water. There was water inside the jug!

She reached for it with her head. Sadly, the jug's neck was too narrow. To get the water to flow out, she pushed the jug down. Unfortunately, the jug was, as usual, too heavy.

The crow pondered for a moment. Then she looked around and saw a few pebbles. A bright idea came to her. She began picking up the pebbles one by one and dropping them one by one into the jug. As more and more pebbles filled the jug, the water level rose. Soon, the crow was able to drink it. She had succeeded.

"Try hard enough and you may soon find the solution to your problem."

Chapter 14

PRIORITIZE WORK, NOT DREAM

A milkmaid was on her way to sell milk from her cow. While carrying the large jug of milk on her head, she began to imagine everything she could accomplish after selling the milk.

Using that money, I'll raise a hundred chicks in my backyard. I can sell them at a good price at the market when they grow up."

She continued to walk, dreaming, "Then I will buy two goats and raise them nearby.". After they have reached adulthood, I can sell them at a higher price!"

The dreamer reflected on the future, as she said to herself, "I'll buy another cow soon, and I'll have more milk to sell. Then I'll make even more money."

In the midst of these happy thoughts, she began skipping and jumping. Suddenly she fell.

Her jug broke and milk splashed onto the ground. She sat in a heap and cried.

"The chickens should not be counted before they are hatched."

Chapter 15

THINK POSITIVE OF YOURSELF

"The Pencil Maker put the pencil aside before he put it into the box.

He gave the pencil five important tips before he sent it into the world. That way he could become the greatest pencil possible.

Firstly, you will be capable of doing many great things if you let someone hold your hand.

Secondly, you will need sharpening from time to time in order to become a better pencil.

Thirdly, "any mistakes you might make can be corrected."

Fourthly, "What's inside will always be your most important part."

Fifthly, on any surface, you must leave your mark. No matter what the condition, you must continue to write."

The pencil understood and promised to remember, and it entered the box with a purpose.

It is now replacing you with the pencil. Be the best you can be.

One: "If you allow God to hold you in His hands, you can accomplish many great things. Give others a chance to appreciate you for your many gifts."

Two: "Every once in a while you will undergo painful sharpening, but it will serve to make you stronger."

Three: "You are going to be able to correct any mistakes you make."

Four: "Your innermost self will always be what matters most."

Five: "You must leave your mark on every surface you walk over. Whatever the situation, you must continue to carry out your responsibilities."

This parable about the pencil should encourage you to know that you are special and you are the only individual capable of fulfilling your purpose.

“Embrace change and never allow your life to become insignificant.”

Chapter 16

OUR PARENTS LIKE TREES

There used to be a huge apple tree. A little boy loved to play under it every day. He climbed to the treetop, ate the apples, and took a nap under its shadow. He loved playing with the tree, and the tree loved him back. Over time, the little boy grew up and stopped playing around the tree every day.

The boy came back to the tree one day, looking sad. The tree invited the boy to play.

"I'm not as young anymore, I don't play around trees anymore." the boy replied.

"I want toys," he added. "I need money to get them."

'I don't have money, but be sure to pick my apples so that you can sell them." Then you will have money.

"The boy was very excited. He grabbed all the apples from the tree and left. After picking all the apples, he never returned. It was sad for the tree.

One day, the boy who had now become a man returned and the tree was thrilled.

The tree invited him to play.

"I have no time to play," he replied. I need to work to support our family. A house is necessary to shelter our family. Could you help me?"

"I am sorry, but I do not have a house. However, you can chop off my branches if you want to build your house. So the man cut all the branches and went home. Although the tree was glad to see him happy since then the man has never returned. It was once again alone and sad.

The man finally came back one summer day, and the tree was delighted. ”Come play with me some more!" said the tree.

”I'm getting older. Taking a cruise will help me relax. Do you have a boat that I can borrow?” asked the man.

„Use my trunk to make your boat. Go sailing far away and be happy. The man then cut the tree trunk to make a boat. However, he did not come back for years.

At last, he came back after many years. "I'm sorry, boy.". But I have nothing to offer you. It said, "No apples for you." The man responded, "No problem, I don't have any teeth to bite into."

"No trunk for you to climb on." "I'm too old for that now," the man answered.

"Without my dying roots, I really can't give you anything," the tree said with tears in his eyes.

“I need nothing else at this point; just some space to rest." “After all these years, I'm tired," replied the man.

"Fine! Tree roots are the best place to rest." "Come sit with me and rest." The man sat down, and the tree was happy and happy, smiling with tears.

“Everyone can relate to this story. Trees are like our parents. As a child, we loved to play without our parents. As we grow up, we leave them, only returning when we need something or when we are in trouble. No matter what, parents will always be there to make sure that you are happy.

It is true that all of us treat our parents the same way as the boy does to the tree. Then we realize how much they do for us when it's too late and we take their generosity for granted.”

Chapter 17

MOTHER IS ANGEL

Once upon a time, there was a child about to be born. The child asked God, "They told me that you were going to send me to earth tomorrow. But how will I live there, being a small child and so helpless? "God replied, "Among the many angels I have selected one for you. She will take care of you when you arrive.

'Why do I do anything else here in Heaven except sing and smile?' said the child. This is what I need to be happy! "God responded, "Your angel will sing for you every day. Your angel will send you love and joy."

Moreover, the child asked, "How am I to understand what people are telling me if I don't understand the language they speak?" "No problem", God said, "Your angel will speak to you the most beautiful and sweet words you will ever hear, and with much patience and care, your angel will teach you how to speak." As the child looked up at God, he asked, "And what would I do when I wanted to communicate with you? " God smiled at the child and said to him, "Your angel will teach you how to pray."

The child said, "I heard there were bad men on earth. Is anyone going to protect me? "God replied, "Your angel will defend you at all costs!" In response, the child spoke sad words: "But I will always be sad since I will not see you anymore." God replied, "Your angel will always keep talking to you about me and will teach you how to return to me.

"At that moment, Heaven was filled with peace, but voices could already be heard from Earth.

In a hurry, the child asked softly, "Oh God if I am about to leave now, please tell me my angel's name!" God Replied, It is not important what name you call your angel... just call her MOTHER!

"Mother is a real God gifted angel in this world."

Chapter 18

DEAREST AND NEAREST MOTHER

One day, a mother duck was on her way to the lake with her little ducklings. It must have been very enjoyable for the ducklings to follow their mother while quack-quacking.

Suddenly, the mother duck saw a fox in the distance. Her face was frightened and she yelled, "Children, hurry over to the lake!" A fox is near!"

All of the ducklings rushed towards the water.

Their mother was uncertain what to do. Walking back and forth dragging one wing on the ground, she began to shuffle backward and forwards.

Seeing her, the fox became happy. He thought to himself, "She must be hurt and unable to fly!" It's easy to catch and eat her!" Then he started running toward her.

As the mother duck fled, the fox followed. The fox followed the mother duck. He would no longer be able to harm her ducklings. Her mother duck saw her ducklings in the lake and saw that they had already reached it. Feeling relieved, she stopped and took a deep breath.

As the fox closed in on her, the mother duck quickly spread her wings and raised herself into the air. When she landed in the middle of the lake, her ducklings immediately came to her.

Upon seeing the mother duck and her ducklings, the fox was in a state of disbelief. Since they were floating in the middle of the lake, he could not reach them.

"Children, some birds drag one of their wings when they see an enemy coming. The enemies think they are injured this way. The children have time to flee if the enemy follows them."

Chapter 19

HELP OTHERS TO FEEL HAPPY

A few years ago, nine athletes with physical or mental disabilities lined up at the starting line of the 100-yard dash at the Seattle Special Olympics.

As soon as the gun went off, they all bounded towards the finish with a relish for winning the race. One little boy, however, tripped on the asphalt, tumbled over a couple of times, and began to cry. Everyone heard him cry. Everyone slowed down to look at him. Every one of them turned around and walked back.

One girl with Down's syndrome kissed him and said, "This will make it better." Afterward, everybody linked arms and walked to the finish line together. In the stadium, everyone stood, and the cheers lasted several minutes. The memories of those who were there are still vivid.

"How come? Since deep down us all know the same thing: What matters most in this life is more than simply winning for ourselves. It matters in this life to help others win, even if that means slowing down and changing our direction."

Chapter 20

MOTHER IS THE BEST

A little boy came up to his mother one evening in the kitchen while she was cooking dinner and gave her a piece of paper that he had been writing on. He read this after his mom dried her hands on an apron, and it said:

'For cutting the grass: $5.00
Cleaning up my room this week: $1.00
Going store for you: $.50
Babysitting my younger brother while you went shopping: $.25
Garbage pickup: $1.00
Accomplished my schoolwork: $5.00
Rake the yard and clean it up: $2.00
Total due: $14.75
When his mother looked at him standing there, the boy could see the memories flash through her mind. Her pen fell to the ground, and she turned over the paper he wrote on and wrote:

During the nine months, you grew inside me; I carried you free of charge.

I won't charge you for all the nights I've sat up with you, prayed for you, and doctored you.

For all the trials and tears you've caused me over the years: No Charge.

In appreciation for all the worry, I knew what lay ahead, for the sleepless nights filled with dread: No Charge.

Toys, food, clothes, even wiping your nose: No charge.

Adding it all up, the cost is No Charge.

Having read what his mother had written, the boy wept as he looked up at his mother and said, "Mom, you're the best."

“Taking the pen, he wrote the following: "PAID IN FULL.”

Chapter 21

PAID IN FULL

A young man was preparing to graduate from college. He had been admiring a beautiful sports car for months in a dealer's showroom, and knowing his father could afford to buy it, he told him that that was all he wanted. As graduation approached, the young man waited to hear from his father that the car had been purchased. His father called him to his study on the morning of his graduation.

Having such a fine son made his father proud, and his father told him how much he loved him. The father gave him a box of beautifully wrapped presents. Curious but somewhat disappointed, he opened the box to discover a leather-bound Holy Book. Angry and yelling at his father, he said, “With all your money, you give me a holy book?” He then stormed out, leaving the holy book behind.

For a long time, he didn't contact his father again. After many years, the young man had become a very successful business person. The man was in a beautiful home and had a wonderful family, but he realized that his father was very old and decided to go to him. The man hadn't seen his father since graduation day.

Prior to making arrangements, a telegram informed him that his father passed away and all of his possessions were to be given to their son. It was imperative that he return home and take care of things immediately. He was suddenly filled with sadness and regret when he arrived at his father's house. While searching his father's important papers, he discovered a still new Holy Book, just as he had left it years ago. Opening the Holy Book with tears in his eyes, he began turning the pages. In the reading of those words, a car key dropped from the envelope behind the Book.

There was a tag with the dealer's name, the same dealer who had the sports car he had wanted. The tag included the date of his graduation and the words PAID IN FULL.

“The Lord's blessings often don't come in the context we expect of them.”

Chapter 22

HOW DO I DEFINE A FAMILY?

A father came home late from work, tired and irritated, to find his 5-year-old son waiting for him at the door.

SON: "Daddy, may I ask you something?"
DAD: "Of course, what is it?" replied the man.
SON: "Daddy, how much money do you make an hour?"

DAD: "It's none of your business. "Why do you ask such an absurd question?" the man asked angrily.

SON: "I simply want to know. Just tell me, how much do you make per hour?"

DAD: "For your information, I make $20 an hour."

Oh, the little boy replied as he bowed his head. Looking up at his father, he asked, "Daddy, can I borrow $10?"

His father was furious. "If you asked for that to buy a foolish toy or some other stupid thing, you have no business asking, and you ought to go to bed right now. Ask yourself why you are so selfish. "I work hard every single day to make such childish decisions."

The little boy went quietly into his room and closed the door.
As the man sat down, he became even angrier at the little boy's questions. How dare he ask stupid questions only to make money? After about an hour or so, the man calmed down and started to think: Maybe he really needed to purchase something with that $10, and he didn't ask for money very often.

As the man approached the little boy's room, he opened the door to his room.

Are you asleep, my son?" The man asked. The boy answered, "No, daddy, I'm awake."

"I've been thinking, maybe I was a little too hard on you earlier," said the man. "It's been a long day and I took out my frustration on you. Here's the $10 you requested."

The little boy smiled. "Thank you, Daddy!" He shouted.

He then pulled out a couple of crumpled-up bills from under his pillow.

Seeing that the boy had money already, the man became angry again.

Slowly, he counted out his money and then looked up at his father.

"Why do you want more money when you already have some?" the father asked.

"Because I didn't have enough before, but now I do," the little answered.

Now I have $20, Daddy. Do you mind if I purchase an hour of your time? Would you mind coming home early tomorrow? I'd like to have dinner with you."

You can share this story with someone you like... or even better, give $20 worth of time to someone you love. It's a short reminder of what you've been working on for so long.

It's important not to put off spending time with the people who mean the most to us, the ones close to our hearts.

The company that we work for could easily replace us in a matter of days if we died tomorrow.
However, our family and friends will continue to feel the loss for the rest of their lives. To be honest, we devote more time to our work than to our family. What a foolish investment!

But the moral of the story is: How can we improve our personal and professional lives?

Don't work too hard... and you know that there's a full meaning behind FAMILY?

"FAMILY stands for = (F) ATHER (A) ND (M) OTHER, (I) (L) OVE (Y) OU!"

Chapter 23

REAL WEALTH

A father of a wealthy family traveled to the country with his son one day so that he could see how the poor people live so he could be thankful for his wealth.

They stayed on the farm of a very poor family for a few days and nights.

After they returned from their trip, the father asked his son, “How was it?” “It was great, Dad.” Have you seen how poor people live?” the father asked. The son replied, "Oh yeah, I saw that." „Well, what did you learn on this trip?” asked the father.

The son replied, "I noticed they had four dogs and we had one." We have a pool that reaches to the middle of our yard, and they have an endless creek." “We have imported lighting in our yard, and they have the stars at night.” “Our terrace reaches to the front yard and they have the entire horizon.” “We have a limited piece of land to live on and they have lands that go outside our sight.” “We have workers who serve us, but they serve other people." "We purchase our food, but they produce theirs.” “We have walls surrounding our property to defend us; they have neighbors to protect them.”

His father was left speechless after hearing this. His son added, “Thanks dad for showing me how poor we are.”

“Rich and poor cannot always be verified with wealth”

Chapter 24

ANGER IS A TERRIBLE THING

Several years ago, there lived a little boy who always had a bad temper. He was given a bag of nails by his father, who told him that if he lost his temper he had to hammer a nail into the fence.

On the first day, the boy drove 37 nails into the fence. The number of nails he hammered daily gradually decreased as he learned to control his anger over the next few weeks. It was easier for him to control his temper than to drive the nails into the fence.

The boy finally stopped losing his temper on that fateful day. The boy told his father about it and the father suggested that the boy pull one nail out for every day he was able to hold his temper. After a day, the boy told his father that all the nails were gone. After leading his son to the fence, the father was pleased to see that all of the nails had been removed. The father said, "You've done well, son, but look at those holes in the fence."

"That fence will never be the same." Whenever you say things in anger, they leave scars. You can put a knife in a man and it will come out. Even if you say I'm sorry a thousand times, the wound still exists. Verbal wounds are just as painful as physical ones.

"Family and friends are the most precious gems in life. They encourage you to succeed and make you smile. They always lend an ear, offer praise, and open their hearts to us. Grow your relationships by being kind. So be careful what you say! Don't hurt friendships by being rude."

Chapter 25

TAKE CARE OF YOUR BELOVED PERSON

A frail old man went to live with his son, daughter-in-law, and grandson aged four. It was difficult for him to walk as his hands trembled, his vision was blurry, and he was shaky in his step. The family ate together around the table. However, his deteriorating eyesight and shaky hands made eating difficult. His spoon rolled peas onto the ground as he ate. Upon grasping the glass, milk spilled onto the tablecloth.

The son and daughter-in-law became irritated by the mess. The son said, "We must do something about grandfather.". They set up a small table in the corner because they were tired of their grandfather's spilled milk, loud eating, and food on the floor. While the family ate dinner together, Grandfather ate alone. Since Grandfather had broken a few dishes, his food was served in a wooden bowl. Occasionally, Grandfather had a tear in his eye as he sat alone as the family glanced his way. Even so, the couple's only words for him were sharp admunitions when he dropped a fork or spilled food. The four-year-old endured it all in silence.

The father noticed his son playing with wood scraps on the floor one evening before supper. He asked the child sweetly, "What do you plan to make?" The boy replied, "Oh, I will make a bowl for you and Mama to eat your food in when I am older." The boy smiled and continued working. The parents were left speechless by the words. Tears began streaming down their faces. Despite not saying a word, both knew what had to be done.

The husband guided Grandfather back to the table that evening by holding his hand. Throughout the remainder of his life, every meal was shared with his family. Neither husband nor wife seemed to mind when a fork was dropped or milk spilled or the table cloth was soiled for some reason.

Children are very perceptive. Their eyes always observe, their ears always listen, and their minds always process the information they consume. When they see us provide a happy home atmosphere for family members, they will imitate our attitude. The wise parent realizes that every day, a foundation for the future of their children gets built. Let us be wise builders as well as role models.

“The purpose of life is to connect with people and make a positive impact. Don't forget to take care of yourself and the people you love all the time!”

Chapter 26

EYES OF A FATHER

A teenager lived alone with his father, and they had a very close relationship. His father believed in encouraging his son. Although the son was always on the bench, his father was always in the stands cheering him on. No game was missed by him.

At the time of his entry into high school, the young man was the smallest in his class. While his father encouraged him, he also made it clear that he didn't have to play football if he didn't want to.

However, the young man loved football and decided to stick with it. It was his determination to practice hard every day, and perhaps he would become a senior and play. While in high school, he never missed a practice or a game but remained a bench warmer all four years. Father was always cheering him on, always encouraging him. In college, he decided to try out for the football team as a "walk-on."

Even though everyone believed he could never make the cut, he did. His coach admitted that he kept him on the roster because he always brought his whole self to every practice and that he provided the other players with the spirit and hustle they badly needed. As soon as he heard he had survived the cut, he immediately dialed his father.

His father shared his excitement and received season tickets for all the college games. During his four years at college, this young athlete never missed practice, but he never got to play.

Just before the big playoff game, the coach met him on the practice field with a telegram. It was the end of his senior football season. After reading the telegram, the young man became deathly silent. He swallowed hard and whispered to the coach, "My father died today." Is it okay if I miss practice today?”

Coach put his arm around his shoulder and said, "Take the rest of the week off, son." Don't even think about coming back to the game on Saturday.

During the third quarter, when the team was ten points behind, a quiet young man quietly slipped into the empty locker room and put on his football gear. Seeing their faithful teammate so soon on the sidelines, the coach and his players were astounded.

"Coach, please allow me to play." "I just have to play today," the young man said.

His coach pretended he hadn't heard him. It was impossible for him to play his worst player in such a close game. The young man persisted, and finally, feeling sorry for him, the coach gave in. "Fine," he said. Soon, the coach, the players, and everyone in the stands could not believe their eyes. This little unknown, who had never played before, was doing everything right. He ran, he passed, he blocked, and he tackled like a pro. His team began to triumph.

The score had been tied for a while. The kid intercepted a pass in the closing seconds of the game and ran all the way for the winning touchdown. The fans went wild. His teammates lifted him high in the air. You've never seen such cheering!

The coach, after the stands had emptied and the team had showered and left the locker room, noticed the young man sitting quietly in the corner all by himself. Afterward, the coach told him, "Kid, I believe it's true." You did great! ”

Why are you so emotional? What did you do? In tears, he said to the coach, “Well, you knew my dad died, but did you know he was blind?” The young man gulped hard and forced a smile. "Dad came to all my games, but today was the first time he got to see me play, so I wanted to show him I could do it!"

Chapter 27

STRUGGLE IS A PART OF LIFE

A man discovered a butterfly cocoon. In one day, a small hole appeared; he watched the butterfly struggle to make its way through for several hours. At that point, it seemed to have given up. It looked like it had gone as far as it could and couldn't go any further.

After that, the man decided to help the butterfly, so he took a pair of scissors and snipped off the remaining part of the cocoon. The butterfly was then able to merge. However, its body was swollen and its wings were small and shriveled.

The man kept watching the butterfly because he thought that, at any moment, the wings would enlarge and expand to support the body, which would contract.

But neither happened! In fact, it crawled around with a swollen body and shriveled wings for the remainder of its life. However, it never was able to fly.

What this man did not understand was that the tightly closed cocoon and the struggle to get through the tiny opening were nature's way of forcing fluid from the butterfly's body into its wings so that it would be ready to fly as soon as it had been freed from the cocoon.

"We sometimes need struggles in our lives. The absence of obstacles in our lives would cripple us. We would not be as strong as we could be. Moreover, we couldn't fly."

Chapter 28

CHALLENGE IS BLESSING

In ancient times, a king placed a boulder on a road. He hid himself and waited to see if anyone would remove the huge rock. Several of the king's wealthiest merchants and courtiers walked around it.

Some blamed the king for not keeping the roads clear, but no one did anything to remove the big stone. A peasant came along with a load of vegetables. Upon approaching the boulder, the peasant laid down his burden and attempted to move it to the side of the road. He succeeded after a lot of pushing and straining. He noticed a purse lying in the road where the boulder used to be as he picked up his vegetables.

Many gold coins were in the purse, along with a note from the King informing the person who was responsible for removing the boulder from the road that he should keep the gold. The peasant learned something that many others never do.

"One can improve one's situation by overcoming each obstacle."

Chapter 29

DON'T JUDGE A BOOK BY ITS COVER

Because the shepherd and his dogs kept an eye on the sheep, the wolf was unable to attack them. Then one day it found a discarded sheep's skin, so it put it on over its own pelt and strolled among the sheep. When it became obvious to the lamb that the wolf was wearing sheep's clothing, the lamb followed him. He soon made a meal of her, and for some time he succeeded in deceiving the sheep, and enjoying hearty meals.

"There is more to it than meets the eye"

Chapter 30

ONE SHOULD NOT JUDGE BY APPREANCES

A woman in a faded gingham dress and her husband, dressed in a faded threadbare suit, stepped off the train in Boston and walked timidly into the outer office of the President of Harvard University.

In a moment, the secretary could tell that such backwoods, country hicks had no right to be at Harvard and probably even weren't qualified to be in Cambridge."

The man said softly, "We want to see the president." "He'll be busy all day," the secretary snapped back. "We'll wait," the lady replied.
The secretary ignored the couple for hours in hopes they would eventually give up and leave, but they didn't, and she became frustrated and decided to disturb the president, even though it was a chore she always regretted.

"They'll probably leave if you keep them in sight for a while," she implied to him.

The man sighed in frustration and nodded. It was evidently not realistic for a person of his stature to spend much time with them, but he disliked the sight of gingham dresses and homemade suits adorning the walls of his office.

The president strode toward the couple, stern faced and with dignity.

The lady told him that her son attended Harvard for one year. He loved it there. But about a year ago, he was killed in an accident. Her husband and I would like to create an everlasting memorial to him."

"The president was unmoved... just shocked.

"Madam," he said, gruffly, "we can't put up statues for everyone who attended Harvard and died here. If we did, this place would resemble a cemetery."

"Oh, no," explained the lady quickly. "We don't want to erect a statue."
We thought of giving Harvard a building instead."

The president sighed. Glancing at the gingham dress and homespun suit, he exclaimed, "A building!" Have you ever wondered what a building costs? Harvard has physical buildings worth almost 7.5 million dollars."

The lady was silent for a moment.

Maybe they can be sold now." The president was pleased.

The woman looked at her husband thoughtfully and asked, "Is this all it will cost?"? “Why don’t we start our own?“ Her husband nodded in agreement.

The president's face turned pale from confusion and bewilderment. A few years later, Leland Stanford and his wife settled in Palo Alto, California, and became the creators of Stanford University, their memorial to a son whom Harvard no longer cared about.

“It is simple to judge someone's character by his or her treatment of those who they believe cannot do anything.”

Chapter 31

ALL YOUR ACTONS REFLECT YOUR PERSONALITY

A father and son were walking in the mountains. Suddenly, his son stumbles, begins to hurt himself, and screams:
"AAAhhhhhhhhhhh!"
Suddenly, he hears a voice repeating: "AAAhhhhhhhhhhh!"
Curious, he shouts: "Who are you?"
As the mountain responds, "Who are you?"
He then shouts to the mountain, "I admire you!"."
As the voice replies, "I admire you!"
He yells in anger, "Coward! "He hears the answer: "Coward!" He turns to his father and asks:
'What's going on?' The father smiles as he replies:
„My son, you need to pay attention." Again the man shouts:
"You are a winner!" The voice answers: "You are a winner!"
The boy is stunned, but does not understand. Then the father clarifies:
"People consider this ECHO, but truly this is LIFE. "It reflects you back whatever you say or do.
Our life reflects our actions in a certain way. Creating more love in your heart will bring more love into the world.
To improve your team's performance, improve your own performance.
The relationship holds true for everything in life. Life will give you back everything you have given to it."

"There is no coincidence in your life. It reflects YOU!"

Chapter 32

DESTRUCTIVE WORDS CAN CAUSE DEEP WOUNDS

A group of frogs was hopping contentedly through the woods, going about their everyday activities, when two of them fell into a deep pit. As the frogs gathered around the pit, they tried to figure out what could be done to help their companions. Following their discovery of how deep the pit was, the remainder of the group of dismayed frogs decided that there was no hope and told the two frogs that they should prepare for death.

Rather than accept this terrible fate, the two frogs began jumping with all their might. Several of the frogs shouted into the pit that it was hopeless and that the two frogs would not have been in that situation had they been more careful, more obedient to the frog rules, and more responsible.

Continuing to cry in sorrow, the other frogs urged them to save their energy and to give up as they were already as good as dead. Following several hours of desperation, the two frogs had become quite worn out.

After some time, one of the frogs responded to the calls of his peers. After being spent and disheartened for a long time, he quietly accepted his fate, lay down in the pit, and died as the others watched helplessly. The other frog jumped with every last bit of his energy, in spite of the pain in his body and the exhaustion he was experiencing.

As the companions began a new chant, yelling for him to accept his fate, stop the pain, and just die. The weary frog jumped harder and harder and wonder wonders! He finally sprung from the pit after leaping so high. Thrilled, the other frogs celebrated his miraculous freedom and then gathering around him asked, “Why did you keep jumping when we told you that was impossible?” Reading their lips, the surprised frog replied to them that he was deaf and that when he saw their gestures and shouting, he assumed they were cheering him on. The encouragement he perceived inspired him to try harder and to succeed against all odds.

There is a powerful lesson in this simple story. The words you use can inspire someone and help him or her to make it through their day. Destructive words can cause deep wounds; your words may destroy someone's desire to continue trying - or even their life. The destructive, careless words you speak can diminish someone in the eyes of others, destroy their influence and have a lasting impact on their behavior.

Chapter 33

WEAKNESS ARE NOT BE UDERESTIMATED

It is possible for a weakness to become one of your greatest strengths. As an example, one 10-year-old boy decided to study Judo despite the fact that he had lost his left arm in a devastating car accident.

The boy began learning Judo with an old Japanese master Sensei. As the boy was doing well, he could not understand why the master had taught him only one move after three months of training.
“Sensei,” the boy finally asked, “Shouldn’t I keep learning more moves?” “This is the only move you know now, but this is the only move you’ll ever need to know,” the Sensei answered.

Even though he didn't quite understand, he kept training because he believed in his teacher.

Several months after that, the Sensei took him to his first tournament. The boy surprised himself by easily winning the first two matches. In the third match, the boy found things harder, but after some time his opponent grew impatient and charged; he deftly used his one move to win. Still amazed by his success, he was now in the finals.

His opponent was bigger, stronger, and more experienced than ever before. Initially, the boy seemed to be outclassed. The referee was worried about the boy getting injured and called a timeout. Just as the referee was about to stop the match, the sensei intervened.

The Sensei insisted, "Let him continue."

"After the match resumed, his opponent made a critical mistake: he dropped his guard. The boy was able to pin him instantly. The boy had won the match and the event. He was crowned champion.

On the way home, the boy and Sensei reviewed every move in every match. Then, the boy had the courage to ask what was really on his mind.

He asked, "Sensei, how did I win the tournament with only one move?"

"You won for two reasons," the Sensei replied. "First, you almost mastered one of the most difficult throws in Judo. And second, the only known defense is that your opponent grabs your left arm."

"The boy's biggest weakness had become his greatest strength."

Chapter 34

PRAY UNTIL SOMETHING HAPPENS

When a man was sleeping in his cabin at night, suddenly his room filled with light, and the Lord told him he had worked for him and showed him a large rock in front of his cabin. The Lord instructed the man to push against the rock with all his strength. The man repeatedly did that every day. From dawn to dusk, he hunched over the cold, solid surface of the unmoving rock, pushing with all his might. Whenever the man returned to his cabin at night, he felt exhausted and sore, knowing that his entire day had been wasted.

When the man seemed discouraged, Satan placed the following thought into his weary mind: "you have been pushing against that rock for so long, and it hasn't budged." Thus, making the man think that the task was impossible and that he was a failure. Discouragement and disheartenment set in as a result of these thoughts. Satan asked, "Why to kill yourself for this?"

It will be enough if you put in your time, giving just the minimum amount of effort."

While he had planned to do that, he decided to take his troubled thoughts to the Lord in prayer. Lord, I have put all my strength into doing what you have asked of me. But even after all that time, I haven't budged that boulder by a single millimeter. What's going on? Why don't I succeed?"

Having accepted, the Lord responded with compassion, "My servant, I told you that your task was to push hard against the rock, and you have done that." It was never in my mind that you would move it. Your job was to push. Having spent all your strength, you come to Me feeling defeated. Is that really the case? Take a good look at yourself. It's obvious you've built muscles in your arms, your back is sinewy, your hands are callused due to constant pressure, and your legs have become big and hard.

Through opposition, you have grown much, and your abilities now surpass those that you had previously. However, you have not moved the rock. But as you pushed and exercised your faith, and trusted in My wisdom, you were commanded to be obeyed and push further. That is what you have done. 'Now I, my servant, will move the rock.' Often, when we hear a word from God, we use our own intellect to figure out what he wants, when in fact, what God wants is simple obedience and faith. Do not doubt the power of God's faith, though you know that it is still He who moves mountains.

P + U + S + H stands for = Pray + Until + Something + Happens

Chapter 35

PERSEVERANCE IS THE KEY TO SUCCESS

A creative engineer named John Roebling had an idea to build a magnificent bridge connecting New York with Long Island in 1883. The experts in bridge-building throughout the world thought that Roebling's plan was impossible and told him to forget it. It was impossible. The plan was not feasible. No one had ever done it before.

In his mind, Roebling had a vision for this bridge that he simply could not resist. Deep down, he knew it could be achieved and kept thinking about it all the time. It was only a matter of sharing the dream with someone else. It took him some time to convince his son Washington, an aspiring engineer, that the bridge was feasible.

As the father and son worked together for the first time, they developed concepts on how to accomplish the task and overcome the obstacles. They hired their crew and began building their dream bridge with great excitement and inspiration.

Despite promising beginnings, a tragic accident at the site cost the life of John Roebling after just a few months. Washington was injured and left with a certain amount of brain damage, resulting in his inability to walk, talk, or even move.

We warned them." Crazy men and their crazy dreams." It's foolish to go after wild visions."

Even though everyone thought that the project should be scrapped since the Roeblings were the only ones who could build the bridge, Washington was not discouraged and he remained determined to complete the project, even with a handicap.

Some of his friends were too daunted by the task to inspire and pass on his enthusiasm. While he lay in his hospital room, the sunlight streaming through the windows, a gentle breeze blew the flimsy white curtains apart, allowing him to see the sky and the tops of the trees outside for a moment.

He seemed to have received a message not to give up. Suddenly, an idea came to him. His only option was to move one finger, which he decided to use the most effectively. As he moved this, he slowly developed a communication code with his wife.

He touched his wife's arm with that finger, telling her to call the engineers again. He used the same method of tapping her arm to tell the engineers what to do next. Though it seemed foolish, the project had begun again.

It took Washington 13 years to tap out his instructions with his finger on her arm until the bridge was completed. Today, Brooklyn Bridge stands as a tribute to one man's indomitable spirit and determination. It is also a tribute to the engineers and their teamwork, and to their faith in someone who was considered mad by half the world. As well, it represents the love and dedication of his wife, who continued to decode her husband's messages and instruct the engineers for over 13 years.

It has to be one of the best examples of a never-say-die attitude that overcomes a terrible physical handicap and achieves a seemingly impossible goal.

Many times, when we face obstacles in our day-to-day lives, our hurdles seem very small in comparison to what many others have to deal with. The Brooklyn Bridge shows us that dreams that seem impossible can be realized with determination and persistence, no matter what the odds may be.

"With determination and persistence, even the most distant dream can become a reality."

Chapter 36

VERIFY THE HUMAN POSITIVELY

There was once an Indian water-bearer who carried two large pots, one on each end of a pole hung across his neck. While the other pot was perfect and always delivered a full portion of water at the end of the long walk from the stream to the master's house, the cracked pot only delivered half as much water.

Over a period of two years, he delivered only one and a half pots full of water to his master's house every day.

Obviously, the perfect pot was proud of its accomplishments, perfect for the purpose for which it was created. But the poor cracked pot felt ashamed and unhappy because it couldn't achieve half of the task she was created for.

A few years after experiencing a bitter failure, it contacted the bearer one day near a stream. "I apologize for my behavior." “But why?” asked the bearer.“

Is there something you are ashamed of?”

"I have been able to deliver only half of my load for the past two years because this crack in my side causes water to leak out all the way back to your master's house. Because of my flaws, all of this work is unnecessary and you don't see the full benefits of your efforts. The water-bearer felt sorry for the cracked pot, and so he said, "On the way back to the master's house, please notice the beautiful flowers we see along the way."

As they climbed up the hill, the cracked pot noticed the sun warming the wildflowers on the side of the path, which cheered it up.

After having leaked half its load, it felt bad, and so apologized yet again to the person who carried it.

The bearer asked the pot, "Have you noticed that flowers only grew on your side of your path, but not on the other side?"

This is because I have always known about your flaws, and I have taken advantage of them. On your side of the path, I planted flower seeds, and every day since we began walking from the stream back to the house, you have watered them. These beautiful flowers have been decorating my master's table for two years. His house would not be adorned by this beauty if you weren't just the way you are."

"We all have our own unique flaws. However, it's the cracks and flaws we all have that make our lives together unique and interesting. The most important thing is to embrace each individual for what they are and find the best in them."

Chapter 37

THE CREATOR IS OMNIPRESENT

A man went to a barbershop as usual to have his hair and beard cut. A good conversation began between him and the barber. They discussed a wide range of topics.

At some point, the subject of God came up. Barber: I don't believe God exists as you say." Client: "But why?" asked the client. Well, that's not hard to understand; you just have to go out on the street to realize this. I wonder what would happen if God existed if there were so many sick people? Is it possible to abandon children? If there was a God, there would be no suffering and no pain. "I can't imagine a God who would allow all that." The client hesitated, but he didn't want to make an argument so he remained silent.

The barber finished his job, and the client left. After leaving the barbershop, he noticed a man on the street with long hair and a beard (it had been a long time since he'd had his cut and he looked untidy). After this, the client entered the barbershop once more and told the barber: "You know what? Barbers don't exist."

"How come they don't exist?" the barber asked. "Well I'm a barber, and I'm here to serve you." "No!" - The client shouts "There are no barbers because there would be no people with long hair and beards like that man who walks on the street."

"There are barbers; the problem is people don't come to us." "Exactly! I agree!"- The client replied. "That's the thing. I believe in God, but people don't go to Him or look for Him, so there's so much pain and suffering in the world."

Chapter 38

THE BELIEVER BOY

Shaykh Fath al-Mowsily recounts the time when he saw a young boy walking through the jungle. The youngster seemed to be uttering words to himself. I greeted him with Salaam, and he responded accordingly. I asked, “Where are you going?” He replied, “To Makkah (the house of Allah)." I then asked, “What are you reciting?” “The Qur’an” he responded. My response was, “You are at a tender age, so fulfilling this obligation is not really your responsibility.”

In his words, "I have seen death approach people younger than me and therefore would like to be prepared in case it comes calling on me." I was amazed and said, “Your steps seem small and your destination far.” He replied, “I must take the step, but it is Allah's responsibility to take me there.” I still asked, “Where is your provision and conveyance (means of transport).” He replied, “My faith is my provision and my feet are my conveyance.” I clarified, “I am asking you about bread and water.”

He said, "Oh Shaykh, if someone invited you to their house, would it be appropriate to bring your own food?" I replied, "No!" “Likewise, My Lord invited His servant to His house. Only the weakness of your Yaqeen (belief) makes us carry provisions. Even so, do you think Allah will let me go to waste?” "Never," I answered. Then he left. I saw him in Makkah a short time after that. As he approached me he asked, “Oh Shaykh, are you still of weak belief?”

“The believer finds the Creator.”

Chapter 39

DO NOT BE INDIFFERENT TO PRAYERS

When he was a boy, his grandmother warned him not to pray at this late hour: "My son, you shouldn't wait until this late hour to pray." His grandmother was 70, but whenever she heard the Adhan (call to prayer), she got up like an arrow and prayed. However, he was never able to get over his ego to get up and pray. Whenever he did anything, his Salah (prayer) was the last to be offered, and he prayed it rapidly to get it in on time. His thoughts turned to this as he got up and realized there were only 15 minutes left until Salat-ul-Isha. As soon as he made Wudhu, he performed Salat-ul-Maghrib. While making Tasbih, he was again reminded of his grandmother and embarrassed by how he had prayed. His grandmother prayed with such harmony and peace. While making Dua and making Sajdah, he stayed in that position for some time.

His day had been busy at school and he was so tired. An abrupt burst of noise woke him. His body was sweating profusely. He glanced at the surroundings. The place was crowded. Almost everywhere he looked there were people. Some stood frozen, looking around, others ran from side to side, and others waited on their knees with their heads in their hands. When he realized where he was, he was filled with fear and apprehension.

He felt like his heart was going to burst. The Day of Judgment had come. When he was alive, he had heard many stories about the questioning on the Day of Judgment, but it seemed so long ago. Would his mind have made this up? No, the anxiety and fear he felt were so great he couldn't imagine anything like this. The interrogation was still ongoing. As he ran from person to person, he asked frantically if his name had been called. Nobody answered him. When his name was called, the crowd split in two and made a passageway for him. He was led forward by two people holding his hands. Unaware of the crowd, he walked forward. The angels took him to the center and left him there. Like a movie, he had his head down and his whole life flashed before him. Trying to open his eyes, he only saw another world. People were all helping one another. He saw his father running from one lecture to another, spending his wealth according to Islam. He watched as his mother set a table while a second was cleared for guests at their home.

His argument was, "I was also always on this path." I helped a lot of others. During my life, I spread the message of Allah. I offered my prayers. During the month of Ramadan, I fasted. I followed what Allah commanded. I didn't do anything he told us not to do. He began to cry, thinking about how much he loved Allah. Allah is the only protector of man, and whatever he has done in life will be less than what Allah deserves. The man was shaking like never before and sweating profusely. As he waited for the final verdict, he kept his eyes fixed on the scale. Finally, the decision was made. Two angels holding sheets of paper turned to the crowd. He felt as if his legs were going to collapse. As they began reading the names of those going to Jahannam/Hell, he closed his eyes. His name was the first to be read. As he fell on his knees, he yelled that it couldn't be true, "How could I be going to Jahannam?" My whole life has been dedicated to serving others. The word of Allah has spread to others through me." He was sweating and his eyes were blurred.

Two angels grabbed him by the arms. After dragging his feet through the crowd, they advanced toward Jahannam's blazing flames. He was yelling and wondered whether anyone could help him. While yelling at all the good deeds he had done, for helping his father, for his fasts, for prayers, and for the Qur'an he had read, he asked if none of them would help him. He continued to be dragged by the Jahannam angels. They were getting closer to Hellfire. Looking back, he made these last pleas. As Rasulullah (Sallahu Alaihi Wa Sallam) said, "How clean would a man be if he bathed five times a day in a river? The five prayer acts cleanse a man of his sins." He began screaming, "What about my prayers?" My prayers? My prayers?" The angels would not budge, and they reached the edge of Jahannam. He felt the fire's flames burning his face. He glanced back one last time, but he had no hope left and was hopeless. An angel pushed him in. He fell towards the flames. Just as he was about to fall five or six feet, a hand grabbed his arm and pulled him back. He raised his head and saw an old man with a long white beard. As he wiped some dust off himself, he asked, "Who are you?" The old man answered, "I am your prayers."

You are so late! Why are you here so late? I was almost burned in the fire! It was you who saved me at the last minute before I fell in." The old man smiled and nodded his head. „You always tended to perform me at the last minute, didn't you?" Instantly, he blinked and raised his head from Sajdah. He was a nervous wreck. He listened to voices outside. The adhan for Salat-ul-Isha was heard. He got up quickly and performed Wudhu.

"Perform your prayers at the right time."

Chapter 40

WORDS SHOULD BE ALIGNED WITH ACTIONS

Once upon a time, there was a boy who loved sweets. Every time his father gave him sweets, he would ask for more. Sadly, his father was poor. He couldn't always afford to give his son sweets. But the little boy did not get the point, and he demanded sweets all the time. The boy's father wondered how to stop the child from eating so many sweets. At that time, there was a very holy man living close by.

The boy's father came up with an idea. He decided to take the boy to the great man so that he could convince him to stop asking for sweets all the time.

The boy and his father went to the great man together. A father asked him, "Would you please ask my son to stop asking for sweets I can't afford?" The great man was in difficulty because he loved sweets. It would be difficult for him to encourage the boy to stop asking for sweets. According to the holy man, he told him to bring his son back after one month.

During that month, the holy man abstained from eating sweets, and when the boy and his father returned after a month, the holy man said to the boy, "My dear child, will you stop asking for sweets that your father cannot afford?"

From then on, the boy no longer asked for sweets.

As the boy's father asked the saint, "Why did you not ask my child to give up asking for sweets when we came to you a month ago?" The saint replied, "How could I ask a boy to give up sweets when I myself love sweets. In the last month, I quit eating sweets." An individual's actions are much more powerful than his words. If we ask someone to do something, we must also do it ourselves. It would be counterproductive to ask others to do things we are not going to do ourselves.

"Keep your words and actions in sync at all times."

Chapter 41

VALUABLE THINGS ARE HIDDEN

"I was wearing a white tank top and a short black skirt, if I recall correctly. As an Orthodox Muslim, I had never worn such revealing clothing in front of my father before. A chauffer took me and my sister Laila up to my father's suite as soon as we arrived.

As usual, he hid behind the door waiting to scare us. During the day, we exchanged as many hugs and kisses as we could. Our father regarded us attentively. A few moments later, he sat me down on his lap and told me something I will always remember. When I looked into his eyes, he said, "Hana, everything that God made valuable is covered, and it's hard to get to." How do you find diamonds? Deep in the ground, protected. Where do pearls come from? At the bottom of the ocean, covered in a beautiful shell. How do you find gold? At the bottom of the mine, covered with layers and layers of rock. You have to work hard to reach them.

"His eyes held serious interest in me. " A human body is sacred. It is important to protect you like diamonds and pearls."

"You are far more precious diamonds and pearls."

Chapter 42

WHAT IS LOTTED CANNOT BE BLOTTED

A Doe had the misfortune of losing one of her eyes, so she couldn't see anyone approaching her from that side. Consequently, to avoid any danger she would always feed on a high cliff near the sea, looking towards the land with her sound eye. By this means, she was able to see whenever the hunters approached her on land and often escaped. But when the hunters found out that she was blind in one eye, they rented a boat, rowed under the cliff where she used to feed, and shot her from the sea. With a dying cry, she cried, "Ah."

“Your fate cannot be changed.”

Chapter 43

THE CLEVER BIRD

Several years ago, there was a bird in a cage singing for her merchant owner. Her song delighted him day and night, and he served her water in a golden dish as a token of his love for her. Before departing for a business trip, he asked the bird what she wanted: "I will walk through the forest where you were born, past the birds in your old neighborhood. Would you mind sending them a message?"

The bird replied, "Tell them I'm in a cage, full of sorrow, singing my captive song." My heart is full of sorrow all the time. I hope I will soon see my friends again and be able to fly freely through the trees. Bring me a message from the forest that will give me peace of mind. Oh, I long for my Beloved, to fly with him and spread my wings. As long as I cannot enjoy all the joys of life, there will be no satisfaction for me."

The merchant rode on his donkey through the dense forest, listening to the birds' songs. At the forest where his bird came from, the merchant stopped, pushed his hood back, and called, "O birds!" Greetings to all of you from my pretty bird trapped in her cage. She has a message for you and wants to tell you about her plight. Please respond in a way that will ease her pain. Because of my love, she is confined with bars on every side. It is as though she is wishing to leave me and sing her songs with her Beloved, but I would miss her beautiful song and cannot let her go."

When the merchant finished speaking, all the birds listened. Suddenly, one bird shrieked and jumped from a branch to the ground. Immediately, the merchant froze. This amazed him more than anything else. A bird had fallen to the ground and died! The merchant went on to trade in the city. He eventually returned to his home. He didn't know what to say to his bird when she asked what message he brought. He stood before her cage and said, "Oh, nothing to say here." She cried, "I must know immediately!"

"I don't know what happened, replied the merchant. "I informed them of your message." One of them fell down the ground and died." Suddenly, the merchant's bird shrieked and fell on her head to the bottom of the cage. This horrified the merchant. In despair, he wept, "Oh, what have I done?" He sobbed, "What have I done?" Now my life has no meaning. I have lost my moon and my sun. I have lost my bird as well."

Opening the cage door, he reached in and gently took the dead bird into his arms. "I have to bury her now," he stated.

As soon as he lifted the bird out of the cage, she swooped up, flew out the window, and landed on the nearest roof slope. She turned to the merchant master and expressed her gratitude, "Thank you so much for carrying my message." "That bird's reply informed me how to gain my freedom. All I had to do was die. I gained my freedom when I died."

"And now I will fly to my Beloved, waiting for me. Goodbye, goodbye, my master is no longer with me." "She taught me the secret; she was a wise bird," the merchant reflected.

"You must be prepared to give up everything to be with the ones you love, even your life itself. And then, you will win your heart's desire."

Chapter 44

FOOLISH TALK

In Nasreddin's district, some wise men were searching for answers to some of the great questions of the time. Their quest brought them to seek out the wisest man in the area. Nasreddin was brought forward, and a large crowd gathered to hear him. Initially, the first wise man asked, “Where is the exact center of the earth?”

Nasreddin replied, "It's under my right heel." “How can you prove it?” inquired the first wise man.
Nasreddin replied, "Measure and see if you don't believe me."

”The first wise man had no answer to that, so the second wise man asked. “How many stars are present in the sky?” he replied. Nasreddin replied, "As many as the hairs on my donkey.".

"What evidence do you have for that?” responded the second wise man.

Nasreddin replied, "Count the hairs on my donkey if you do not believe me."

"That's silly talk," said the other. "How can you count the hairs on a donkey?"

Nasreddin replied, "Well, how can one count the stars in the sky?"
"If one is foolish talk, then the other is also foolish talk.” The second wise man was speechless.

The third wise man was becoming irritated with Nasreddin and his answers, so he said, “I see you know a lot about your donkey, so can you clarify to me how many hairs there are in its tail?”

“Yes,” responded Nasreddin. There are just as many hairs in its tail as there are in your beard."

"How can you confirm that?" asked the other.

I can confirm it without any problem,” replied Nasreddin. “I will pull one hair out of my donkey's tail for everyone you pull out of your beard. I will admit that I was wrong if the hairs on my donkey's tail do not come to an end at exactly the same time as your beard."

Obviously, the third wise man was not willing to do this, so Nasreddin was declared the winner.

“Don't argue about everything.”

Chapter 45

APPRECIATE OLD THINGS

Nasreddin told his friends one day: "If I die, bury me in an old grave." "Why?" his friends wondered. "Because", he continued, "If the angels come, I will tell them that I have already died and been questioned many times, and then they will return from where they came."

"Old things are very useful in time."

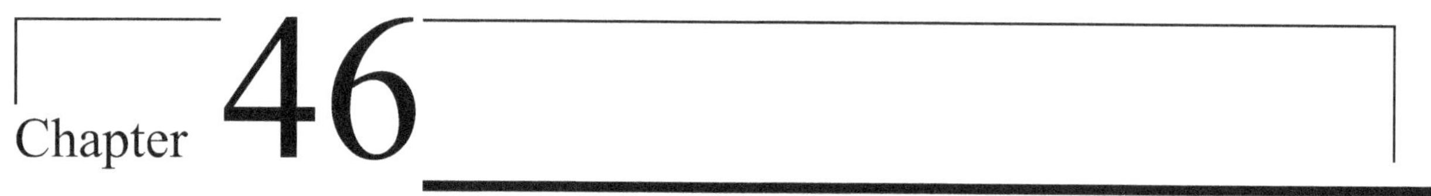

Chapter 46

THE BRILLIANT BOY

A man on his way to the market carried two sacks of wheat in the saddle of his donkey. He was tired after a short time, so they sat under a tree for a little while. After waking up from his nap, he couldn't find the donkey and searched everywhere for it. While walking, he met a boy. He questioned the boy, "Have you seen my donkey?" The boy asked, "Is the donkey blind on the left eye, lame on the right foot, and carrying wheat?" The man was glad and responded, "Yes, exactly! Where did you see it?" The boy replied, "I didn't see it." The man was angry and decided to punish the boy by taking him to the village chief.

The judge asked, "My dear boy, if you hadn't seen the donkey, how could you describe it?" The boy replied, "I saw a donkey's tracks, and the right and left tracks were different from one another. I understood that the donkey passing there was limping. In addition, the grass on the right side of the road was eaten, but not the grass on the left. Based on this, I assumed that his left eye was blind. Wheat seed were scattered on the ground, and I presumed he was carrying a load of wheat. The judge understood how clever the boy was and told the man to forgive him.

"We learn from this story not to judge people too quickly."

Chapter 47

RESULT OF EXTREME CUNNING

During a beautiful spring morning, a merchant loaded his donkey with bags of salt and went to the market to sell them. Together, the merchant and his donkey walked to the market. They had not walked far when they came to a river on the road.

Unfortunately, the donkey slipped and fell into the river, and the salt bags he carried became lighter as a result.

The merchant had no choice but to return home and load his donkey with more bags of salt. Having now deliberately reached the slippery Pery riverbank, the donkey fell into the river and wasted all the bags of salt on its back again.

The merchant discovered the donkey's trick immediately. After returning home, he reloaded his donkey with bags of sponges.

The foolhardy donkey began its journey again. When it reached the river, he fell into the water once more. His load did not become lighter this time, but heavier.

Laughing, the merchant said, "You foolish donkey, your trick has been uncovered.

“People who are too clever sometimes overreach”

Chapter 48

LAZY PEOPLE CANNOT ALLEVIATE POVERTY

A colony of ants was busy drying some damp grains of corn during a cold, frosty day in the middle of winter.

There was a grasshopper half-dead and hungry who came up to one of the ants. In a faint voice, he requested a grain or two from your corn store to save his life.

We worked day and night to bring this corn into the store. “Why should I give you my own food?” the ant asked irately. "What were you doing last summer when you were supposed to be gathering food?”

The grasshopper said, "I don't have time for things like that. I'm too busy singing to carry corn about."

The ant laughed bitterly. "As far as I am concerned, you can sing all winter for me," he said. He turned back to his work without saying a word.

In every religion, we are taught to help the less fortunate. But it also teaches us that we must work hard and not rely on the kindness of others to survive day to day.

Chapter 49

THINK AND THEN WORK

Once upon a time there was a fox who was hungry and looking for food. His stomach was very empty. Despite his best efforts, the fox couldn't find food. At last, he reached the edge of the forest and searched there for food. He suddenly noticed the hole in a big tree.

There was a package inside the hole. It made the hungry fox very happy to think that there might be food in it. The fox jumped into the hole and when he opened the package, he saw that it was filled with food, bread, meat and fruit!

A woodcutter in the forest had placed food in a tree trunk while he was cutting down trees. He planned to eat it for lunch.

The fox eagerly started to eat. Having finished eating, the fox felt thirsty so he decided to leave the trunk and drink water from a nearby spring. The problem was that no matter how hard he tried, he was unable to escape from the hole. Would you like to know why? It is true that the fox had eaten so much that his size made it impossible for him to squeeze through the hole.

This caused the fox much sadness and upset. As he said to himself, "I wish I had thought a little before jumping in."

"Yes brother, this is what happens when you don't think carefully about what you do."

Chapter 50

TRUTH MUST WIN

A long time ago, roosters ruled over cats in Africa. Cats worked all day to gather food for the roosters, and at night they brought it all to the roosters. The rooster king was always taking all the food for himself and the other roosters.

The roosters loved eating ants. Thus, every cat wore a purse around its neck, which it filled with ants for the rooster king. The cats were not happy about the situation. They wanted to rid themselves of the king so that they could take control of the food they had gathered through hard work and hardship. But they were scared of the roosters.

Cats had been told that roosters' combs were made of fire, and that if cats disobeyed them, they would burn! The cats believed them, so they worked from early morning until late at night for the roosters.

However, one night the fire in Mrs. Cat's house went out. She asked her kitten to bring some fire from Mr. Rooster's house. When kitten entered the rooster's house, she saw that Mr. Rooster was fast asleep, with his stomach swollen from having eaten ants. The kitten was afraid to rouse the rooster, so she went home empty handed. She then told her mother what had happened.

In response to that, Mrs. Cat advised, "Now that the rooster is sleeping, pull out some dry twigs and put them near his comb." Once the twigs catch on fire, bring them home." The kitten collected dry twigs and brought them to the rooster. He was still sleeping. Although the kitten placed the dry twigs near the rooster's comb fearfully, they did not catch fire.

Despite her efforts, the kitten kept rubbing the twigs on the rooster's comb but it didn't work; they wouldn't catch fire.

The kitten returned home without having made any fire, and told her mother, "The roost's comb does not set twigs on fire." Mrs. Cat asked, "Why can't you do anything right?" "Come, let me show you how to make fire with the rooster's comb." They together approached Mr. Rooster's house.

As of yet, he was asleep. Mrs. Cat placed the twigs as close as she could to the rooster's comb. However, none of the twigs caught fire. Then, trembling with fear, she put her paw near the rooster's comb and carefully touched it. She was surprised to find that the comb was not hot, it was very cold, and it was just a red color.

In the moment that Mrs. Cat realized that the roosters had lied to the cats about their combs, she ran out and told all the other cats about the tricks that the rooster was playing. Following that day, the cats were no longer employed by the roosters.

Initially, the king of the roosters was very angry with the cats and threatened to burn all of their houses unless they worked for him!

"But the cats said, "Your comb does not contain fire. It just has the color of fire." We touched it while you were sleeping. We discovered that you lied."

The king of the roosters fled when he found out that the cats knew he had lied to them. Nowadays, when roosters see a cat, they scurry away, since cats still terrify them.

"Lies cannot be covered, the truth will be revealed one day."

THE END

Thanks for finishing these stories.

www.ingramcontent.com/pod-product-compliance
Lightning Source LLC
LaVergne TN
LVHW080555160826
845677LV00010B/1866